IN T

IN THE STILLNESS

Jock Anderson

alpha

Copyright © 1999 Jock Anderson

First published in 1999 by Alpha

05 04 03 02 01 00 99   7 6 5 4 3 2 1

Alpha is an imprint of Paternoster Publishing,
PO Box 300, Carlisle, Cumbria, CA3 0QS, UK
http://www.paternoster-publishing.com

The right of Jock Anderson to be identified as the Author of this Work
has been asserted by him in accordance with the
Copyright, Designs and Patents Act 1988

British Library Cataloguing in Publication Data
A catalogue record for this book is available from the British Library

ISBN 1-898938-82-2

Cover Design by Mainstream, Lancaster
Typeset by WestKey Limited, Falmouth, Cornwall
Printed in Great Britain by Caledonian International
Book Manufacturing, Glasgow

For our children and grandchildren

Contents

Acknowledgements   ix

Foreword by John Stott   xi

Abbreviations   xii

1 In the stillness   1

2 Approaching the Bible – the gift of your
   Friend   8

3 The practicalities   20

4 Prayer in the stillness   33

5 When you pray   40

6 The face of the King   51

Notes   61

Acknowledgements

Let me mention that this little book has an antecedent. In the 1950s I was asked to rewrite and edit some articles in a Christian student magazine, and the authors of each article gave me their full permission to use any or all of that material. It related to forming the habit of a daily devotional time. The result was a small book entitled *The Quiet Time*. That joint venture, published by the InterVarsity Press enjoyed a wide circulation in many languages. More recently the question arose of updating that book, and Jenny Taylor suggested that I undertake this.

The present book is a call to a wider age range, to give urgent attention to this same subject. I myself owe a huge debt of gratitude to many friends over the years, beautiful people who have encouraged me to follow Jesus Christ every single day, and especially to keep that quiet part of the day 'in the stillness' with the Father. I want to say thank you to Jenny for her initial prompting and for her constant backing of this present writing. The completed manuscript was read by family members, and by friends of various ages and backgrounds, and I am deeply grateful for their suggestions. I particularly want to thank my dear friend John Stott for writing the foreword. I acknowledge that in this I am very greatly honoured.

Last and most felicitously I wish to thank my beloved wife Gwendy who gave time to setting the material in order and without whom this could neither have been written nor published.

Foreword

I have enjoyed Jock Anderson's friendship since I first met him as a schoolboy of 16, soon after his conversion. We then kept in touch during his student days when he served as a medical missionary in Pakistan and Afghanistan, and during recent years in which he has endured much disability and pain with extraordinary courage and trust.

So I can testify that *In the Stillness* is an authentic expression of his Christian faith and life. He protests, albeit with characteristic gentleness, against the noise and pressures which threaten to crowd our intimate times of daily communion with God through Christ by the Spirit.

He grounds everything he writes in Scripture, and refuses to acquiesce in the spirit of the age. He demonstrates that Bible reading and prayer are an indispensable part of discipleship. But he does more than challenge us. He shows us that these disciplines should grow naturally out of our relationship of love with the Lord Jesus.

Readers will find Jock Anderson honest and understanding about the problems. He also gives us a lot of practical advice from his long and wide experience.

John Stott

Abbreviations

KJV = King James Version
OT = Old Testament

1

In the stillness

'FIRST THINGS FIRST'. Out in China earlier this century Isobel Kuhn posted up a card in her room as her daily reminder: 'God first'. For her it was a call to devote the first hour of her day to meeting with God. In the stillness of the dawn she read her Bible, and she waited on God in prayer. This was her daily habit, which shaped her to become a most relevant teacher, author and example to thousands of Christians down the years. The same has been true of countless others, known and less known, for whom this devotional habit has led to new personal freedom and life.

What has happened to us? Have we all but lost this precious practice? Or has it already completely disappeared? The kaleidoscopic advances and changes in this century have been accompanied by ever greater pressures on our personal time. Stillness is hard to come by, and for many it isn't even wished for. Constant noise has become preferable. Some people actually fear silence because they find it too painful. Life for many has increasingly become a rat race, or just a daily juggling to try to meet all the demands and deadlines. The need for some personal space and stillness has become very widely felt. Today, the relief of stress is an in-subject. But what sort of relief and what sort of stillness? The call to stillness which this book explores has a specific objective. It is directed to all who want to orientate their lives to a closer relationship and friendship with Jesus Christ. It is a call to practice a twin approach to Bible study and prayer, which is at the very heart of the inner life of Christian discipleship. It describes that meeting in the stillness with God, which can set the tone for the whole day. Such a meeting may be for only five minutes, and it may have to be at night if the morning is too rushed. But it focuses on God's word in the Bible, his love and his presence, in which our lives become increasingly centred and less stressed. Doing this is not a vestige of the past. All around the world the number of followers of Jesus Christ is on the increase. He is eternally alive and he is still entering the lives of those people who turn to him.

What a discovery

'Can I come in?'

'Who are you and what do you want?'

'I am Jesus. I just wanted to say "Hello" and have a chat with you. Is that OK, or are you busy now?'

'You are Jesus? Are you the Jesus who died on the Cross? And you really want to talk with *me*?'

'Yes, I'm that one. And, yes, I did die on the cross – for you, because you are very special to me.'

'How can I possibly be special to you, Jesus? There's nothing in me worth dying for.'

'But I died for you because I love you. I want your friendship and I want to be a real friend to you. Do you understand what I'm saying?'

'O Lord, please come in. I'm sorry I was so slow to welcome you.'

It really is like that with the Lord Jesus. He is gloriously alive and he is here with us. He actually wants our friendship and our devotion. People in the Bible as well as down through history have discovered this amazing fact. You may perhaps remember that Abraham was called the Friend of God. Abram (later named Abraham) and his wife were given the staggering promise that in their very old age they would be given a son and descendants through whom *the whole world would be blessed.* Abraham really took that on board, and waited and finally saw the promise come true. God was so pleased because here was a man who believed and trusted him without hesitation. No wonder he was called the Friend of God (see, for instance, 2 Chronicles 20:7; Isaiah 41:8; James 2:23). God had not found many willing to trust him like that, but here was one who did.

In the New Testament, Jesus calls his disciples 'friends' (Jn. 15:15) because he shared things with them. One or two of his twelve early disciples were especially close to him, for example John – 'the disciple Jesus loved' (Jn. 13:23; 19:26; 21:7,20). What do you think puts a person in that special category? It seems it was those who wanted to be close to him ('reclining next to him' Jn. 13:23), who wanted to hear his words (like Mary, Lk. 10:39–42), and wanted to obey him (Jn. 14:23). Today there are

numbers of Christians who really love Jesus and
who want to serve him with their whole hearts; who
long to know him in a deeper, more personal way
and to share their lives with the living, risen Lord
Jesus.

I was first introduced to Jesus Christ by a school
friend who had himself been led to Jesus by other
school friends. It was the most unforgettable experience of my life and the wonder of it is that it didn't
stop there. After asking Jesus if he would become my
Saviour and Lord, I found there was a new reality in
my life. Jesus Christ was alive. He was with me and,
as my school friends had said, he was a Friend who
has promised never to leave or forsake me (Heb.
13:5). My RE teacher never taught me that! Now I
learned that life was a kind of daily walk with him.
The man who explained to me most clearly how this
relationship with Jesus begins, once wrote a booklet
called *How to Succeed in the Christian Life*. It started
with the sentence: 'The Christian life is like riding a
bicycle. If you don't go forward, you fall off' – a simple but very helpful way of saying that the Christian
life is a progress. It involves growth, development,
movement forwards. It is a growing relationship
with Jesus which requires to be worked at and
strengthened, in order to be all that God intends it to
be. As in marriage some people give up without
putting too much effort into it, so in the Christian life
some people seem to forget that it is a relationship
which requires self-giving input from the Christian's
side. Self-giving input, among other things, is discipline, and discipline doesn't come naturally to us. It
often includes suffering. Yet that is a spontaneous

part of a true love relationship. It is what leads us to give Jesus the offering of our time.

Time for your friend

As friends of Jesus, one of the most important disciplines is that of spending a daily time alone with him. Jesus did it on earth (e.g. Mark 1:35); and before ever he appeared on earth, he lived in the closest relationship and harmony both with his Father in heaven and with the Spirit of God who was to come into the world. So his followers down the ages, especially those greatly used by God, have cultivated this daily time with him. Do you want to be that kind of Christian? Then you *must* spend time alone with him.

Within a few days of my becoming a believer, I was taught the importance of doing this daily. I found that all my Christian friends had made a habit of praying and reading their Bible every day, even those who led very busy lives. This very year that I write, one of the busiest men I have ever known, Professor Verna Wright of Leeds General Infirmary died of cancer. He was held in high honour in Leeds, both as a brilliant scientist and as a Christian communicator. During his time at Leeds he produced more than 1,000 scientific papers, some 1,200 other technical communications and wrote or co-authored 21 books, 19 dealing with research, clinical practice or training. He originated multi-disciplinary research in bioengineering. I could go on. He initiated United Beach Missions, and was in great demand as a preacher. With nine children in his home you would have to say by any standard that he was a busy man! You wouldn't expect him to have much time for prayer every day. However his eldest son told me that his father used to spend one hour every day alone first thing in the morning at the kitchen table in prayer and Bible study. According to the *Guardian* 'Obituary' a unifying link can be found for his science and religion: '. . . both are driven by a *profound compassion* for humanity' (my italics). But Verna would take us another step back and say that he received his compassion for humanity from the Lord through his regular *prayer and meditation on the Bible*.

Reinstating that time of stillness with God

I want to examine with you the relevance and the urgency of getting back to this stillness. I want to look with you at the twin elements for this time – a feeding on the Bible through which the Lord instructs us, and prayer in which we speak to him and listen to him and come to know him. This short book explores the ingredients we choose as well as the problems we encounter when we decide to persevere in keeping this time of stillness with the Lord. The rewards in doing this are so very great.

But, you may reasonably argue, not all of us can keep a daily time of stillness. All sorts of pressures come upon us. Take the case of Sarah with her often absentee husband and three under-five kids. A 'quiet time' for her? You must be joking! All right, we shall come to her problem in chapter 3. Most of us are bombarded by different demands and pressures. This will mean that our times for quiet will vary in length. But nothing need actually deflect us. His love beckons us all. Today, many who are disillusioned, *are* searching for spiritual reality and the deepening of their Christian faith.To give time to prayerful reading of the Bible, and to opening ourselves to the truth and love of our Lord, brings him into focus and we discover the Bible as our true Friend's love letter to us. In the next chapter we shall further examine our whole approach to the Bible.

2

Approaching the Bible – the Gift of Your Friend

The Bible is a truly remarkable book, unique in a number of respects: It is still the world's best seller and there is a demand for it in some countries so huge that it simply cannot be met, even though the distribution of Scriptures in some form or another amounts to *well over half a billion annually*. This phenomenal demand for the Bible can only be accounted for because of the nature of the book. It has a *unique message* which connects with human need. It brings hope and healing to our world in all its heart-breaking spiritual bankruptcy. It is not, as is sometimes supposed, a description of 'man's search for God' . On the contrary, it describes God's search for the heart of man, with the offer of what the Bible terms free salvation: I have loved you with an everlasting love; I have drawn you with lov-ing-kindness. (Jer. 31:3). Again, 'For God so loved the world that he gave his one and only Son, that whoever believes in him shall not perish but have eternal life. For God did not send his Son into the world to condemn the world but to save the world through him' (Jn. 3:16,17). A God who reaches down to man with such a free offer of forgiveness and salvation is unique in the religions of the world. This amazing news is to be found alone in these Scriptures. It is a composite message, progressively built up by the different writers, but seen in all its fullness and wonder in the Bible taken as a whole. That is its central message: a *unique person – Jesus Christ* given to us through the love of God.

Other approaches

This positive appraisal of the Bible is in sharp contrast to the attitudes of some Western theologians and critics. It is a tragedy that many of these critics of the Bible adopt their stance for reasons of their own. One common reason is *ignorance* of its contents. A second reason is *prejudice*, perhaps based on political correctness. It is not considered 'politically correct', for example, to teach in schools and even in some churches that the Bible is the word of God. But I would suggest that a major reason is a *refusal to obey* what God says about putting him first in our lives and loving our neighbours as ourselves. On these two commands the Bible is absolutely uncompromising. A fourth reason is *hostility* to the Bible's call for our exclusive worship of the God and Father of our Lord Jesus Christ. That again is a politically sensitive issue in a multicultural society.

It must be said that there are many others who do not share this downgrading of Scripture. Through no fault of their own they have grown up with a complete absence of Bible teaching. What they do pick up is the way the media present the Bible – which can often be condescending, derogatory and ridiculing. Never has the need been greater for our Western society to be reacquainted with the Bible's teaching. With that I return to the subject of the Bible's authorship.

The Bible's dual authorship

The two verses quoted above (Jeremiah 31:3 and John 3:16,17) were written by men, yet clearly bring a message directly from God himself expressing his love for mankind. This illustrates the Bible's unique claim to have a *dual* authorship. It is written by human beings; yes, of course. But it is also written by God. This is stated more specifically in some Scriptures. For example, Peter wrote, 'No prophecy of Scripture came about by the prophet's own interpretation. For prophecy never had its origin in the will of man, but men spoke from God as they were carried along by the Holy Spirit.' (2 Pet. 1:20,21). The Jewish people recognised that the holy Scriptures were of divine origin. They were people of the Book. Paul in the New Testament put this in a striking and vivid way. He wrote, 'All scripture is *God-breathed*' (2 Tim. 3:16). The human authors were not puppets or typewriters. All their God-given nature, personalities and natural gifts were harnessed in the writing of Scripture. God *breathed* through them his message. And it is the message they were given which you and I have to find and receive. Our approach to that is vital, because it is possible to hear the human writers quite easily and yet entirely miss what God has to say to us – one pitfall we can stumble into all too easily. We need ears to hear, as Jesus himself stressed. His message is highlighted by the apostles and indeed by Jesus himself in the following significant verses: 'These things are written that you may believe that Jesus is the Christ, the Son of God, and that by believing you may have life in his name' (Jn. 20:31). 'For everything that was written in the past was written to teach us, so that through encouragement of the Scriptures we might have hope.' (Romans 15:4). It is written: 'Man does not live on bread alone, but on every word that comes from the mouth of God' (Mt. 4:4).

Spiritual life and sustenance, hope for the future, self-control and a sense of personal responsibility are just some of the benefits that come to us when we respond to the message of God's word. A radical transformation begins to take place in us. Indeed the Bible is not only of human authorship. It is of dual authorship.

Three other pitfalls to avoid

At this point there are other pitfalls to watch out for. People use the Bible in all sorts of ways of their own choosing and according to their own traditions. In order to be able to deepen our relationship with Jesus through reading the Bible, we need to know what to avoid as well as what to go for. Primarily the Bible's purpose is to affect the way we live rather than just to have an aesthetic or academic appeal.

So watch out to see if you are being lulled by the language of the Bible. Some years ago a large volume was published, entitled *The Bible Designed to be Read as Literature*. Yes, our Authorised Version happens to have been translated at a time when the English language was rich and perhaps at the zenith of its beauty – a circumstance for which we may well be grateful. The Old Testament has sublime passages in it. Certainly it is helpful to be able to appreciate the various genres of Old Testament writings, the historical, the poetical, etc. We can say that the Greek of Luke was literary and that of the Epistle to the Hebrews highly polished. But the fact is that other New Testament writers used the Greek of everyday speech. It was not primarily 'designed' to be read as literature. The practical purpose of the Bible, OT as well as NT, is to *change our lives*, not just to appeal to our aesthetic tastes. The Bible is not primarily there to help us to get a PhD in religion but a living personal relationship with God; not to make us clever but to make us 'wise for salvation' (2 Tim. 3:15).

A further pitfall relates to our attempt to search the Bible for answers to questions that it does not even discuss, let alone answer. This has caused a good deal of confusion in some people's minds. Take for instance the question of the origin of the human race. What light does the Bible cast upon this question? In the first place it does not teach the precise mode of creation. However it does make some very important statements: first, that we were created by God, we were, in fact, the pinnacle of his creative work, derived from two sources: the 'dust of the

earth' (i.e. meaning whatever material God used)
and the 'breath of God', so making man a 'living
soul'; secondly, we were created in God's image and
likeness, with moral and spiritual qualities, among
others, which distinguish human kind from all other
created beings; thirdly, we were given authority to
rule over the rest of creation, to be, as it were, God's
stewards and deputies in running the earth
smoothly according to the laws he laid down for our
benefit and happiness; fourthly, we were created to
have fellowship with God, to worship him, love him,
serve him, and 'enjoy him for ever' (in the words of
the *Shorter Scottish Catechism*). The fact is that the
Bible does not use Western technological language.
It is addressed to people down the ages in every part
of the world. The sometimes metaphorical language
that God chose was to enable *everyone* to understand.
And generally, throughout the world and down
through history, they have done so. It is mainly simple, clear and unsophisticated, and we do well to
handle it that way.

Another pitfall is an over-concentration on the
record of the Bible as a preserve of archaeological
and historical evidence. Of course it is that, an amaz-
ingly preserved and fascinating resource for those
studying in these areas. But in summary, the Bible is
more than an historical document to be preserved.
And it is more than a classic of English literature to
be cherished and admired. It is a record of God's
dealing with human beings, of God's revelation of
himself and his will. The Bible carries its full message, not to those who regard it simply as a heritage
of the past, or who praise its literary style, but to

those who read it, so that they may discern and understand God's word to man.

The purpose of the Bible – essentially practical

So, let me say again that the books of the Bible primarily have a practical, not an academic purpose; that is to say the revelation of God in the Bible is intended to affect every aspect of human living, not only our intellectual enquiry. King David does not only say, 'The Lord is my light'; for mere illumination as an end in itself was never God's purpose. But he says rather, 'The Lord is my light *and my salvation*' (Ps. 27:1). The light was given to show the way. It was to bring in a new way of life, with a new power and purpose for living, i.e. for a practical, and not just an academic purpose. The Apostle Peter reminds us that it was the salvation of our souls about which the earlier prophets had written in the Scriptures and that the Holy Spirit in them was testifying to the sufferings and glory of Christ, the Author of that salvation (see 1 Peter 1:9–12). John expressly states that the purpose of his writing the gospel was 'that you may believe that Jesus is the Christ, the Son of God, and that by *believing you may have life in his name.*' His purpose was not purely academic, but practical, vital, 'down to earth' for directing our life down here, in order to bring us 'up to heaven'. Again, Paul does not tell Timothy that the Holy Scriptures will merely make him wise; but 'wise for salvation' (2 Tim. 3:15) for this is God's purpose (1 Thess. 4:3).

He also commends the elders of the Ephesian church 'to God, and to the word of his grace, which can build you up and give you an inheritance among all those who are sanctified' (Acts 20:32). Millions of Christian believers have proved down the ages and are proving today that it is this word of God's grace which is the means of bringing us to know God in this life and to be built up in him. That is its purpose; that is why God has given us his word and why he has so wonderfully preserved its transmission down the years.

This theme is well summed up in the words of Deuteronomy 29:29: 'The secret things belong to the Lord our God: but the things revealed belong to us and to our children for ever, that we may *follow* all the words of this law.' The Bible has a *practical* purpose.

The focus of the Bible

We come now to the focus of the Bible. Since the purpose of the Bible is a practical one, the salvation of mankind, we should expect to find that the focus of the Bible is on the One in whom that saving relationship is centred. And this is precisely what we do find, for the focus is on Jesus Christ. The whole Bible is centred on him. To the unbelieving Jews he himself said: ' "You diligently study the Scriptures because you think that by them you possess eternal life . . . If you believed Moses, you would believe me, for he wrote about me. But since you do not believe what he wrote, how are you going to believe what I say?" '

In The Stillness

(Jn. 5:39, 46, 47). Again, to the two disciples on the resurrection afternoon, he said, ' "How foolish you are, and how slow of heart to believe all that the prophets have spoken![1] Did not the Christ have to suffer these things and then enter his glory?" And beginning with Moses and all the prophets, he explained to them what was said in all the Scriptures concerning himself' (Lk. 24:25–27); and later to the eleven and others that very evening, ' "Everything must be fulfilled that is written about me in the Law of Moses, the Prophets and the Psalms." '[2] (Lk. 24:44). It is thrilling to trace through the Bible 'those things which concern the Lord Jesus Christ' (Acts 28:31, KJV) from Genesis 3:15, the earliest prophecy concerning Christ as the offspring of the woman, to Revelation 22:20, where his last promise is given; to see, for instance, in the book of Esther how wonderfully God preserved the ancestry of Christ from the results of an international edict to exterminate all Jewry; to sit at the feet of Isaiah as he unfolds the appalling sufferings of Jehovah's Servant and his subsequent triumph; to share with the 'beloved disciple' those treasured intimacies in the life of Jesus, and indeed to open one's heart to all that these men of God had been shown by the Holy Spirit of the 'sufferings of Christ and the glories that would follow'. In truth this is the study of a lifetime as we respond to his love and as daily, we, like Mary of Bethany, 'sit at the Lord's feet listening to what he says.' (Lk. 10:39). Jesus Christ is God incarnate, God in human form, God who came to us, and through whose death we find true inward deliverance and freedom, in this world and the next.

In view of all this, it is urgent for us to keep check-ing out our approach to the Bible. There are three conditions we need to fulfil when we come to read it.

1. *We must come with an open mind and with intel-lectual honesty.* There are none so blind as the wilfully blind and there are none less likely to learn from Scripture than those who come with their minds already made up. To the Pharisees who said, 'Are we blind too?', the Lord had to reply, 'If you were blind, you would not be guilty of sin; but now that you claim you can see, your guilt remains.' (Jn. 9:41). Now the Pharisees were those who nullified the word of God by their tradition (Mk. 7:13). But our preconceived tradition can often do the same. It can make our Bible reading utterly fruitless because we come to it 'knowing' everything already. Because we say 'we see', therefore our guilt remains. However, if we come with humility to learn, he will teach us as he promised (Mt. 7:7), and the things which are hidden from the 'wise and learned' (the intellectually self-sufficient) will be again revealed to little children (Lk. 10. 21).

2. *We must come with surrendered wills.* The path of discipleship will involve a cross for each one of us. It will mean saying gladly to our heavenly Father 'Not my will, but yours be done'. It is our great privilege to tread the path the Master took. What use is it, for example, if we agree theoretically that we should love our neighbour as ourselves and yet remain unwilling to do so? God requires more of us than the mere assent of our minds to his word. He demands the wholehearted consent of our wills. Indeed, the unwillingness to obey God's revealed will is the

biggest cause of spiritual blindness in the world
today (see Jn. 7:17). So when we approach the Bible
we must come with a readiness to act on whatever
God asks us to do. ' "Whoever has my command-
ments and obeys them," said the Lord Jesus, "he is
the one who loves me. He who loves me will be loved
by my Father, and I too will love him and show
myself to him." ' (Jn. 14:21).

3. *We must come with faith to believe.* 'Anyone who
comes (to God) must believe that he (God) exists'
(Heb. 11:6). Faith is an absolutely indispensable
condition in our approach to God. He desires that we
believe him utterly and trust him implicitly. The
simple, unquestioning trust of the tiny child is what
delights his heart – which, of course, is why he
exhorts us to become 'as little children'. Faith, in fact,
is the response of the human heart to a God who is
infinitely worthy of our trust. Hudson Taylor, a great
missionary pioneer in China, used to point out that
the words 'Have faith in God' (Mk. 11:22) could be
rendered, 'Hold the faithfulness of God'. In other
words, the emphasis is on the worthiness of the One
in whom we place our confidence. This puts faith in a
completely new light. It is seen to be not so much a
virtue to be admired as a response to be expected.
But more than this, faith is a response that is
demanded. 'Have faith in God' comes as a command. Faith, then, is a matter of deliberate choice.
When Jesus saw disease he responded with sympa-
thy. But when he saw lack of faith, he countered with
a rebuke. ' "O unbelieving and perverse generation,
how long shall I stay with you and put up with
you?" ' (Lk. 9:41). To the unbelieving Jews he said,

' "If you do not believe that I am [the one I claim to be], you will indeed die in your sins." ' (Jn 8:24). It is a sin not to believe. That is why the writer to the Hebrews stresses that 'without faith it is impossible to please God'. (Heb. 11:6).

How then can I strengthen my faith? For some this may be plain sailing. But for others it is an extremely hard question. In the sense that faith is a relationship, it is much more difficult for those to develop faith whose parenting may have left them with no sense of belonging or identity, but rather a personal alone-ness like a wilderness, and an inability to trust. The reality of the Fatherhood of God is meaningless for many people. As well as being encouraged to read the Bible, they need to be loved and understood and prayed with. For all of us the way to strengthen our faith is by learning more about the wonderful triune God who inspires our faith. St. Paul writes, 'Faith comes from hearing the message, and the message is heard through the word of Christ.' (Rom. 10:17). The more we study the Bible and hear him speaking to us, the more we shall believe him and the more we shall love him. A life of real intimacy with our loving Saviour is the prize that comes to those who believe. And what a prize that is!

So then we must come to him with humility to learn, with surrendered wills to obey, and with faith to believe. In the next chapter we turn to the practicalities of making Bible reading part of our daily stillness with God.

3

The practicalities

Before and until the love of Jesus becomes real to us, much of the reading of the Bible may seem difficult to understand, even boring and irrelevant. But when the Spirit of Jesus has moved in our lives, and we recognise him as that unique God-man who has given us new life, then, starting with the gospels, the words of Scripture turn into his love letter to us. When we are in love with Jesus, we have a brand new desire to be near him and to hear his words to us. Can you remember a time when you used to exchange letters with a dearly loved person who was far away from you? We usually go to some quiet place if we have a love letter that we want to read. It is so special, so longed-for, and touches us so deeply. It brings close the one who wrote it to us. When we are in love with Jesus the same sort of thing happens. We will want to find a quiet place and time when we can meet with him. Many Christians have called this their 'quiet time'. It becomes the most important part of their day, even if it is a short time. Some may meet with God in this way twice, or perhaps even three times, every day, like David and Daniel (see Psalm

55:17; Daniel 6:10). It becomes as much a part of their day as breakfast, lunch and supper. But the comparative silence of Scripture on the number of times we should spend in this way each day can only mean that it is a matter between us and God.

As a rule the 'quiet time' should be a *daily* time. Making a habit of it has the advantage that it becomes a part of one's mind set. It belongs to one's whole way of thinking. If we have a day without it, something is somehow missing. Does this mean that our fellowship with God is just a matter of getting into a *daily habit* of Bible reading and prayer? No, not at all. But the habit helps to open a door which then makes it easier for that closeness to develop. What we mean is this: Setting aside that time every day is like saying to God,'Here I am. May we talk together? I have put aside this time because you have called me to do so. It is for you, Lord.' Does that make sense? As James wrote, 'Come near to God and he will come near to you.' (James 4:8) If we decide that we *don't* have time for God, then can we really expect him to talk to us, to meet with us? Hardly, though he well might do so in his grace and mercy. However, we cannot *expect* him to, if that is our attitude. Remember, it is those who seek him with all their hearts who find him (Jer. 29:13).

A morning time for stillness

As has already been indicated, the Bible gives strong support for a *morning* time of quiet.[3] There are in fact a number of good reasons why most of us should ideally observe it in the morning. Here are the main ones:

1 The example of the Lord Jesus. 'Very early in the morning while it was still dark Jesus got up and went to a solitary place to pray' (Mk. 1:35).
2 The frequent allusions to the morning time in the Old Testament.
3 The experience of numberless Christians down the ages.
4 The appropriateness of beginning a day *for* God *with* God. Sadly it is often because we are not sufficiently committed to live *for* him that we fail to spend time *with* him.
5 Freshness and freedom from distraction before the newspaper or the postman arrives.
6 That precious silence before the buzz of the day's activities.

Do you find it difficult to get up early? (Who doesn't?!) You have to be motivated enough. Actually, God works to get you up. Your Heavenly Father seeks your worship (Jn. 4:23,24). The awesomeness of this is great. It is the expulsive power of a new affection, which helps you to go to bed a bit earlier, in order to be able to get up earlier. It can be done. Remember the orchestra. It tunes up *before* the concert, not after it is over. The athlete limbers up *before* the race, not after it is over. Tuning up and limbering up belong before, not after the event. It is highly suggestive that God gave the Israelites their daily manna in the wilderness early every day. 'In the morning you will be filled with bread. Then you will know that

I am the Lord your God' (Exod. 16:12). 'Each morning everyone gathered as much as he needed, and when the sun grew hot, it melted away' (v. 21). Jesus showed that this manna was in fact a type (i.e. a picture portraying something yet to come) of himself, the true Bread of God 'who comes down from heaven and gives life to the world' and that we must feed on him by faith. In other words, we grow daily as we feed on him daily. And, incidentally, he who said, 'Give us this day our *daily* bread', also said to Satan, when he was exceedingly hungry, 'It is written: "man does not live on bread alone, but on every word that comes from the mouth of God".'

We are so privileged to be called by our Lord to come and seek his face. Suppose the phone rings. It's a call from Whitehall! The leader of your country has invited you *personally* to a special function. Whew! You may find that the date clashes with something else you had planned for that day. What will you do? You will cancel or postpone your previous plans and accept the invitation humbly and gratefully and you will go without question. What an honour you have been given! Exactly. And does not the very same reasoning apply to God's gracious invitation to us? He calls to us to meet with him every day. 'He wakens me morning by morning, wakens my ear to listen like one being taught' (Isa. 50:4).

Other difficulties

And what if there isn't silence and stillness? What if someone's TV or radio is already blaring? One

practical solution can be ear plugs! It also helps if we
are able not to resent our neighbours' noises too
much. They may be lonely and need the radio's com-
panionship, or have problems which the TV helps to
distance for a while. They have to block out stillness
because they cannot bear it. If you ask for grace to
understand them and then pray for them you may
find your *resentment* has gone, which is so often the
major component in the distraction that their noisy
habits cause you. It is hard to read the Bible and pray
if you're bitter or hopping mad!

Another type of external hindrance is the sort that
Sarah faces. Listen to her: 'I've got three kids, all
under the age of five years. My husband has a job
that keeps him away from home for weeks at a time.
Nowadays, I do not know what stillness means until
after nine o'clock at night, and by that time I just
want to flop. I may relax in front of the box and then I
go to bed, only to be woken up by the baby who is
teething and won't settle.'

What would be God's response to Sarah? I can
guess what it is not. It is *not* likely to be the following:

'Sarah, your husband should be at home helping
you. Why is he away so much?'

'Sarah, you shouldn't have had so many children,
so close together . . .'

'Sarah, who comes first in your life, do I or does
your family? Remember, I said "anyone who loves
his son or daughter more than me is not worthy of
me' (Matthew 10:37)." '

'Sarah, you are not going to be an effective Christian, not if you don't have a daily "quiet time". No

way! Let's be honest: you really are a bit of a failure, aren't you?'

All that does *not* sound like the voice of our Lord.

I think the Lord Jesus would say something more like the following:

'Sarah, it must be difficult for your husband to be away so much, knowing what a cost it is for you. He is working very hard in order to support you and the children.'

'Sarah, you are doing so well to cope with those three kids the way you do. I am really proud of you.'

'Sarah, I am glad you love your children so much. When the work seems overwhelming I want you to know that I am here with you. I will never leave you. When the littlest one is screaming and you feel like screaming yourself, just tell him that I love him and give him a hug from me, yes and have another hug for yourself for the wonderful care you are giving to those demanding kids of yours! We'll love them together, Okay?'

'Sarah, don't feel that at this stage our love for each other depends on your having a "quiet time". We can still tell each other, "I love you" even under all the pressures of the day. Remember that I am with you all the time and so is my love for you. As for the pressures, well, I have known them too, and I under-stand completely. Set aside time for me later, and I will be there.'

(If you haven't found all that in the Bible, I suggest you read it a bit more!)

Sarah has a common and very real problem which is not solved just by telling her that Jesus loves her. She probably believes that already, though it helps to reiterate it, of course. But there are other things she can do: first, maybe she could *share her problem* with another Christian mum, and learn to get mutual help from that source. Then perhaps they could *have each other's children* for a break from time to time – on a regular basis so that once a week Sarah could be free to *pray with a friend* and be refreshed; she could work at learning to *talk with Jesus* throughout the day about everything that is happening all around. She could *keep a verse constantly propped up* in the kitchen or wherever, and let it soak in. She might be surprised how it helps to sing about the house; and it would be great if she could also pray over her children, especially at night. Well done, Sarah!

Hearing God's word

We come now to an important and interesting question: how do we actually *hear* God speak in our Bible study? Mary sat at Jesus' feet listening to what he said (Lk. 10:39). We can't literally sit at his feet in a physical sense, much as we may long for that. But Jesus stated: ' "My sheep hear my voice" ' (Jn. 10:27), and he assured his followers that they would hear him. Because we are made in God's image we all have moral awareness, we have a conscience which God uses. And we have within our spirit a 'place' where his promised Spirit comes and lives and enables our hearing. We learn to know his voice.

That is an immensely strengthening thing when it happens.

Jesus also spoke about stages of hearing. He himself from his childhood was versed in hearing the Scriptures read in the synagogue, and for us this corresponds with our getting acquainted with the Bible, its books, authors, periods of history and message. Hearing and reading and learning the Scriptures becomes our inner storehouse, out of which Jesus through his Spirit can speak directly to us. For the Bible is no ordinary book. Jesus said that his words are spirit and life (Jn. 6:63). This means that the Holy Spirit lights up a truth, a promise, a command, and speaks it specifically into our consciousness. This is powerful like a sword, and we are enlightened and guided. We hear the Lord with the ears of our heart, as he said we would. We don't live by bread alone, but by every word that proceeds (today) from the mouth of God.

But note that we only hear what he is actually saying to us when we come receptively, and humbly and obediently. Remember that we come to the Bible to meet the divine Author, and to hear his voice. He will speak to us about many things, including our ambitions, our money and our relationships. He does this in our very highest interests, if only we can recognise and accept that. But it becomes harder and harder to hear him if we resist him, in whatever area. If we have tasted that the Lord is good we will long to hear him, and surrendering to his will won't be such a struggle. We will taste more of his love for us and that will nourish our lives.

The word of God nourishes us

Yes, the Bible provides a huge variety of nourishing food. God will feed us if we come hungry to meet him, to listen to him, to take on board what he says to us. St. Peter reminds us, 'Like newborn babies, crave pure spiritual milk, so that by it you may *grow up* in your salvation, now that you have tasted that the Lord is good.' (1 Peter 2:2). The writer to the Hebrews reminds his readers that *mature* Christians need solid food. It is God's wonderful provision for his people that daily prayer and Bible reading should be the means *par excellence* whereby his children grow strong and mature, and daily become more like the Lord Jesus. The essential of spiritual nutrition is the receiving from God of his word by his Spirit – the word that makes Christ real to us. It is the written word received into our hearts which brings to us the living word of God, the Lord Jesus Christ. He is called the Word of the Father. He is God's manna to be eaten every day. Jesus said, ' "I am the bread of life. Your forefathers ate the manna in the desert, yet they died. But there is the bread that comes down from heaven, which a man may eat and not die. I am the living bread that came down from heaven. If a man eats of this bread, he will live for ever." ' (Jn. 6:48–51). Yes, we eat sacramentally too. This is included, but always with faith. 'Believe, and you have eaten' sums it up.

Perhaps I should ask myself, how hungry am I for Jesus? What do I really know about hunger? In the summer of 1971 I was visiting the town of Chakcharan in the highland plateau of central

Afghanistan. It was the third year of such a severe famine that many humans and animals had died of starvation. The first day I was there a crowd of orphaned children approached me. They were thin with wrinkled skin – just like very old emaciated people. They called out to me 'We are hungry. Give us food.' They were eating scrub from the parched land all around. That was their only food. It wasn't corn flakes they wanted, or sausage rolls, or fish and chips, or porridge. It was FOOD, just plain something they could eat. Anything, everything, just food. Sadly, no food was available to those starving kids. How different for Christians for whom there is spiritual food in abundance! God offers us food. So often we don't take it, and we become malnourished. All our physical hunger and other needs tend to be so well met that our spiritual hunger is diminished. This makes it much harder for us to desire God's nourishment and to move on in studying his Word. Our lack of hunger may have other causes – exhaustion, depression, or lack of giving out to others. We need patience, and sometimes we need help from others, and we need honesty. To grow into Christ's likeness, we do need to eat the food he supplies and we only do this if we are hungry for him.

Methods of study

Feeding on God's Word leads us to explore different methods of Bible study. There are many helpful books available. For a superb introduction to the Bible, now used in many schools, *The Lion Handbook to the Bible* would be hard to beat. The Scripture Union publishes the classic book by John Stott, *Understanding the Bible*, and, more recently, *The Bible in Outline*, by several authors which provides a concise overview of every book of the Bible.[4] Both books are superb. But first there is the question of Bible translations. There are several very good ones in use today. If you are not familiar with the Bible, use a version (i.e. a translation) you can understand. A standard modern translation is the *New International Version*. The *Good News Bible* is a fresh and popular translation. Some editions of it have the brilliant and helpful line drawings of Anna Vallotton. For reading the Bible *aloud* we now have the *Contemporary English Version* which is superb and highly readable. Some modern paraphrases are also very helpful – perhaps to use as a supplement.

There are good Bible notes available which suggest a passage for each day and explain any difficult words and verses. I would recommend the excellent *Scripture Union Notes* geared to different age groups and needs. The valuable *Bible Reading Fellowship*'s notes, Selwyn Hughes' *Every Day With Jesus*, and many other Bible study helps are also available in the shops. You may find it helpful occasionally to read the whole Bible in one year, that is, about three and a half chapters a day; and also to do more in-depth *topical* studies if you can find the time. Most people don't want to get tied to one method for too long. It is important to find the one which is in keeping with your own background and gifts and stage in life. Choose what really nourishes you. After going through the passage ask yourself, what does the passage say? Secondly, what did it mean to its first readers? And thirdly, how does the passage apply to me? This needs to be honest. It includes a heart response as well as a head response. The Scripture Union expands these questions as follows: 1) what is the main point of this passage? 2) What does it teach us about God? 3) Is there a promise or a command, a warning or example to take special notice of? 4) How does the passage help us to understand ourselves, our situation or our relationships? Expect God to speak. God's Spirit moves, and if you are open, will communicate with you directly. It may be a joyful application – or some completely new understanding or discovery – a delighted 'Aha!' of new realisation. Or it may be a fresh conviction of wrongdoing with a call to repentance in some very specific form. In some of the Scripture Union's notes there is the following suggested way of responding:

'Turn your discoveries about God into worship and your discoveries about yourself into a fresh resolve to do what God says. Decide how to share your discoveries with others in word and action.'

You may wish to keep a journal to remind you about what God is showing you. Many find it very helpful to keep this kind of spiritual diary.

It is vital to store God's word in our hearts, so do consider memorizing Scripture regularly if you can. And in passing, consider learning by heart the order of the Bible's books: Genesis, Exodus, Leviticus . . . Jude, Revelation. This makes it much easier to look up a Bible reference. Some families used to learn the list at breakfast time until it became known by heart!

This really is a valuable aid to our learning and studying, all the more because these days there is a great deal of ignorance of Scripture. Meditating on a Scripture passage, soaking ourselves in it, is another excellent way of allowing God's word to dwell in us richly (Col: 3:16). Our roots go down deeper. As we persevere, the love and friendship of our Lord Jesus Christ through his word will truly be life-changing.

This now brings us to the subject of prayer. Our searching of Scripture can easily become purely academic if it is not soaked in prayer. The two are complementary and need to be inseparable. We study on our knees, figuratively if not literally. This is because we study in order to be mastered by the Lord of Scripture, not just to master the Scriptures themselves. In the following chapter we look at prayer in more general terms, and try to understand why it is so essential, and sometimes so difficult.

4

Prayer in the stillness

How do Bible study and prayer fit together? Although we are looking at them consecutively, they belong together in our life of discipleship. When our Bible study is done in a spirit of humble prayer it comes alive; our prayer in turn needs to be informed and given content from God's revelation of himself in the Bible. The Scriptures tell us who God is, what he is like, what he has done for us, and what he wants us to pray for. The greatest prayer warriors – to use an old word for them – are the men and women who have proved God's trustworthiness, and achieved so much through their prayers. They know intimately what God is like, the things he is interested in and the requests he longs to answer. They know God, and they pray accordingly. For example, George Müller knew that God loved children, especially orphaned children. He set up several orphanages in Bristol. He needed money. He wanted to honour God, so he decided to pray and never to ask any human being for the money, only God. The money came, and in remarkable and thrilling ways the needs of this growing work were met, directly through George

Müller's and his colleagues' prayers. As a faith
strengthening exercise I recommend anyone to read
that awesome record of God's amazing provision
repeated again and again.[5]

Prayer becomes a great exploration, an adven-
ture, because it takes us beyond ourselves. Prayer is
communication with our God. The mental bound-
aries within which we customarily live can be very
narrow. We easily remain imprisoned in our own
small self-centred world. An old adage says:

> Two men looked through prison bars;
> One saw mud and the other saw stars.

This doesn't just refer to a pessimist and an optimist.
The call to pray means that we have the option of
looking up rather than down. We can choose to see
not only the stars, but we can reach out to the awesome Creator who made the stars. Prayer is amazing
because it actually connects us with what is beyond
ourselves. As we just noted, the link between prayer
and Bible study is the link which will define our
praying. The whole subject is of course vast, and the
large spectrum of books available is very varied. But
this reflects the centrality of prayer. What we have to
guard against is the time we may spend reading
about prayer, rather than actually praying.

With regard to our daily time of stillness, prayer is
the bridge across which we meet with God. We come
because he draws us (Jn 6:44), he seeks us (Jn 4:23), he
calls us by name (Jn 10:3). We come because he has
adopted us into his own family, and has become our
loving Father. We come because Jesus has shown us

the way of obedient listening prayer, which was his own way and is also to be ours. We come to build a deepening faith-relationship. We come to meet the Lord, to worship and thank him for his love shown to us on the cross. We ask him to speak to us in our Bible reading, and we pray for the day ahead. But this isn't as straightforward as it may sound. Deep down we all know that we should be cultivating prayer. But in practice we get diverted and all too quickly stop praying.

But I give up so easily

Enter Steve into the picture. He is a man in his twenties who is lucky to have got a job after leaving university. He says thoughtfully, 'I used to look forward to our prayer times at college. We sang together, we knew each other, we all felt like praying, and it all came easily. Perhaps I'm more tired now and just don't get up early enough. When I do try to pray, it's as though my prayers only get as far as the ceiling. God seems miles away, and I simply give up.'

I am certain that Jesus looks with great love at Steve. He understands him through and through, and wants to encourage him, not judge him. I believe he would speak to him along these lines: 'Steve, I know that praying on your own can be hard. It takes lots of practice and determination, until you know me better. You were glad to pray with your friends at college. Could you find one soul-friend, someone who shares your faith and would start praying with you once or twice a week? And try to go to a church where people love me. If you cut yourself off it's like a coal falling from the burning fire. It loses its glow and becomes black and useless. Take time just for you and me. Is that so very hard? Remember that I am with you, and welcome me, and talk with me.'

But sometimes it is even worse

Steve did find a church that was helpful, and he found a friend who agreed to pray with him. Some time later he came and confided: 'For a while things were so much better. When I had wandering thoughts I was learning to direct them back to Jesus, because I knew he was there. I think I was learning to trust him more. I do believe that he is there and that he welcomes me. But my workplace gets more and more complicated. I was pressed to join the National Lottery club, against my conscience, because I really believe gambling is wrong. And another time I was pressed to sign a claim for expenses in excess of what the four of us actually did spend on that job. They "pushed" me the way people do, and I signed it. And there are other things like that. I just don't feel able to stand up against all the pressures, and prayer gets more difficult.'

I can hear the Lord gently saying, 'Steve, did you think that things would always be plain sailing? The workplace is often difficult for a Christian, especially for one Christian on his own. Don't turn from me. Talk to me about all these things, and let me give you strength to do what your conscience tells you. Keep talking to me and listening to me. And there is something else, Steve. Remember when prayer is difficult that your unseen enemy is trying to keep you from me. I opposed him to his face when I lived on the earth, and so must you. His name is the Slanderer, the Deceiver. He is still around and he still hates me. You have got to resist him in my name, to make him leave you. Don't forget.'

Steve didn't forget. He thought a lot about that, because as it happened he knew some people living near him who were involved in occult practices. Steve was curious at first but then reacted strongly against their influence. He began to understand that living in the Kingdom of God, under God's rule, would take a tremendous amount of working at, and help from God, because in many respects it was the exact opposite of the secular life that was going on around him. For Steve it was like swimming against the stream. Together with his prayer friend he grew more determined to follow God's word and God's way.

Parable of the Sower

Do we realise what happens in our lives when we don't pray? We can see it in the well-known parable of the sower. The word of God goes in one ear and out the other in those who are stony-hearted. Some more receptive people hear at first and get very excited about God: but before long it all evaporates. There are others who hear God's words and keep them in mind, but oh dear! the influence of their worries or perhaps their many pleasures, or, very topically, the lure of more wealth, bit by bit has the effect of making these people deaf to God. But there are other hearers of God's Word who are also doers of it. They are the ones who prayerfully work at taking notice of what they hear. By his Spirit they repent of their immature ways and follow Jesus more closely. They really act on what they hear, as Jesus instructed, and they grow into fruitfulness.

It is prayerlessness that lets the soil of our lives retain the stones that completely block even the remembrance of what the Lord said. It is prayerlessness that prevents us facing and changing our self-love, instead of allowing Jesus' love to go so deep in us that we are rooted in it. It is prayerlessness that leads to the gradual diminishing of our Christian discipleship, as bit by bit we let other priorities take hold and take over. Lord, teach us to pray. We want to hear you speak to us.

How God speaks

This brings us back again to the question of how God speaks to us. In the previous chapter we stressed hearing (and studying) Scripture as the storehouse out of which we hear God. By his Spirit, God imprints and impresses on us what he wants us to hear. We learn to distinguish and to recognise this communication from him, and to prize it. When we think about it, it is amazing that we actually have a God who speaks. Of all his creation, humans are the only ones made in his image, made to hear and to speak back to him. 'The Mighty One, God the Lord, speaks and summons the earth from the rising of the sun to the place where it sets' (Psalm 50:1).

We now go on to note that he speaks and calls to us in a variety of other ways. His words come primarily through Scripture. They also come to us through his creation, as the beauty and awesomeness of the world he has made testifies to him. Our circumstances will often speak directly from God. We instantly know in our hearts what God is getting through to us. Sometimes a friend says something which resonates inside us as God's word. Some people are directly spoken to through dreams – God has great access to us when we are asleep! Or he may speak through some other working of his Spirit, such as a vision, or a picture, with a meaning and significance which becomes crystal clear to us. It is prayer that opens up to us these riches, as the Spirit of Jesus fills us. Oh how privileged we are to have a God who speaks to us!

' "To whom much is given, of him will much be required." ' (Lk. 12:48). Have you been given much? Then you have all the greater responsibility to pray. There is the world of difference between thinking (and reading) about prayer, and actually praying. It is when we pray, and not otherwise, that God can really equip us and give us what we need for loving him, and following him. In the next chapter we will turn to some practicalities for our daily prayer time in the stillness.

5

When you pray

We start with Jesus's words in Matthew 6:6, 'When you pray, go into your room, close the door and pray to your Father who is in heaven.' Eugene Peterson helpfully paraphrases this verse in *The Message, The New Testament in Contemporary Language*: 'Here's what I want you to do: Find a quiet, secluded place so you won't be tempted to role-play before God. Just be there as simply and honestly as you can manage. The focus will shift from you to God, and you will begin to sense his grace.'[6] Such a lot can happen when we set aside and make use of a quiet place for prayer, a 'room' where we go and shut the door to the outside world. It may be a corner of a separate room, or it may be just a special chair. It becomes our daily meeting place with Jesus. Some people kneel. Some may have a special object nearby which draws them to worship him. Some people find it helpful to light a candle. They wish to wait on God in the stillness, and the flame of the candle is a very powerful symbol, a reminder of God's light that overcomes the darkness, and God's warmth of love which can expel the deep fears in their hearts. Shutting the door to be with God alone has a deep significance. It symbolises our individual preciousness and belonging to our Lord. 'Come away, my love' (Song of Songs 2:10,13) he says to us. He wants us for himself, away from all other distractions. He wants us to picture him right beside us. At other times we can acknowledge him praying for us in the glory of Heaven, and he lifts us up to him there.[7] We truly belong in both places.

Using this precious time

How much time can you give him in the stillness?

If you can only manage ten minutes or less, then you have to cut your pattern according to your cloth. What is most important to you? A short Bible portion which will nourish you during the day? A time of deliberately praising and blessing him, and calling on his Spirit to fill you? He does 'dwell in the praises of his people.' The joy of being with him will make you want to give him more time.

For those who have set aside more time for this morning period of prayer there are several ingredients, each of which the Bible teaches and encourages us to practise. Let us consider the importance of each, and ask the Spirit of God, the one who breathes life into our prayers, to lead us. We summarise these ingredients as, Adoration, Confession, Thanksgiving and Supplication, and we will look at them one by one, so that we can better incorporate them into our praying.

Adoration

With adoration we include worship of the Father and the Son. This is the most important ingredient and the one which is often neglected and found to be difficult. The very first commandment of Moses " 'You shall have no other gods before Me" ' (Exod. 20:3) is a call to adoration and worship. So is the first commandment which Jesus reaffirmed: 'You are to love the Lord your God with heart and soul and mind and strength.' (e.g. Mt. 22:38). Nowadays more churches have brought worship to the fore with their music groups and worship songs. While many people appreciate silence for their worship, we also do well to worship God with singing. Do you worship God with singing? If that would disturb others, then don't! But by all means bless and worship God first of all.

When we adore and worship we have to *know* the person we are approaching. How we address a person depends on who the person is, and on our relationship with him or her. When we worship God, we address the Creator of the universe, the Lord of Hosts, whose name is Holy, from whom our sins have separated us, and who will one day be the Judge of all the earth. When we worship Jesus we adore him as the Son of God and also as caring Son of Man. As God he is far above all; as perfect man he identifies with us intimately. So in our worship we pray, 'Holy and mighty God, you are my close and intimate Friend' (Ps 63:1, paraphrased). We learn to worship him with both awe and intimacy, because both are equally fitting. For some people God remains distant in the highest heavens, almost too awesome to approach. Others appear to worship God with over-familiarity, a 'God's my mate' style. In starting our day with adoring wonder and with loving worship we are so blessed by the Lord, and in doing so our sleepiness, our depression, our reluctances, and also satanic opposition can all quickly be lifted right away from us.

Confession

'Lord, I thank you I'm not like so-and-so' prayed the Pharisee in Jesus' teaching. The Publican went into a corner and cried, 'O God be merciful to me, the sinner.' The closer we draw near to God, realising his perfection, the more aware we become of the sinfulness and the darkness of our hearts. We are convicted of our impurity, as he speaks into our conscience. Like the Publican we must come to God repenting of our sins and seeking forgiveness. We cannot presume to come into God's presence as if we had every right to it. We do not. God is *holy*, which means separate from all that is sinful, impure, evil. We are unholy people who need to be made clean. In his tender mercy God sent the Lord Jesus who achieved that cleansing for us. In giving his life on the cross in our place, he took the totality of sin into himself. Through our confession of our sins and receiving his forgiveness from the cross we are made completely clean. It is wonderful when this first dawns on us and actually takes place.

But we know that there is such a thing as day-to-day dirt from the road, contamination that needs to be washed away. We all know times when we have said something we regret, or seen something that we wish we had never seen, or done what has left us feeling dirty. There are also ingrained wrong attitudes which need to surface and be forgiven. The Apostle John wrote, 'If we claim that we are free of sin we are only fooling ourselves. A claim like that is arrant nonsense. On the other hand, if we admit our sins – make a clean breast of them – he won't let us down; he'll be true to himself. He will forgive our sins and purge us from all wrong doing.' (1 Jn 1:8–9, Eugene Peterson op. cit.) A repentant clean heart knows confidence in prayer. So let us keep short accounts with God. Let us receive his mercy and find grace to help us in our time of need (Heb. 4:16). We don't prosper when we try to cover up our inner darkness. On the contrary our love shrivels up. Jesus made it so plain when he said, 'She loves much because she has been forgiven much.' He said this about a woman who had come confessing her great need and crying at his feet and anointing them with perfume. The same is true of a multitude of people whom Jesus healed, delivered and forgave. They were the ones who then most loved him and followed him. Jesus had given them forgiveness and new life. He still exchanges our sin and darkness for his forgiveness and freedom.

This was my experience. I remember when I was a young doctor in a mission hospital. One hot day I had a row with the senior nurse in that institution. She said something to me in front of others which was rather hurtful in the circumstances. I flared up and replied in a manner I regretted afterwards. I knew that what she had said was true and that she could have picked on many things in my life which would have hurt me even more. What she did say set my heart ablaze with anger. I marched off to my clinic, unable to concentrate on my work, just fuming. The devil seemed to say to me, 'So, you are a Christian "missionary" are you? Teaching these people about the love of God, eh? I think you belong somewhere else, don't you? What are you pretending about?' That evening I went back to my mission bungalow, still bitter over what she had said to me, but even more upset by *my own reaction* and what I had said to her. In the cool of that evening I walked around the bungalow garden trying to pray. I couldn't. I realised that I almost hated this colleague. . . . I saw the cross once again and the Lord bearing all my pride, my temper, my bitterness against Sister Kathleen. I told the Lord that I was quite unable to love her or to ask for forgiveness for my own remarks. 'I can't do it', I moaned bitterly. The Lord seemed to say to me, 'I know you can't, but I can. I died for you both.' I knew I had no choice but to go and say sorry and to ask for her forgiveness. As I looked up to the cross and saw Jesus dying for me suddenly I found myself thinking about Kathleen, about her own tiredness in the summer heat of that place and of all the ways my own attitude hadn't exactly helped her in her own work. I breathed quietly, 'I'm so sorry, Lord.' Then, miracle of miracles, I found I actually loved her! I went to her bungalow and asked if I might speak with her and her husband. They were so warm. In a minute the whole situation had changed and the three of us have been close friends ever since.[8]

In this true story I was not wanting to face an encounter with Jesus on that day because I was not clean. The Holy Spirit mercifully led me back to the cross where I again found that the blood of Christ cleanses from all sin. I was then able to do the right thing and ask for forgiveness. My inner peace and liberty returned. I had applied what the Spirit had already taught me years before. Jesus does not grant us a nice comfortable time in his presence when there is sin in our hearts. No way. 'If I had cherished sin in my heart, the Lord would not have listened' (Ps 66:18)

Thanksgiving

Thanksgiving and gratitude follow the wonderful gift of forgiveness. The Bible is full of it, especially in the Psalms. To be given a gift and not to be thankful for it is a hurtful thing. Why was it that ten lepers were healed by Jesus and only one went back to fall at his feet and thank him? 'Where are the other nine?' Jesus asked. Parents give birthday presents to their children and expect (and normally get) some gratitude. How much more is it right for us to thank our God spontaneously for his forgiveness and his many blessings!

But what about the painful things that happen to people? This is much harder. Again and again the Bible calls us to give thanks in all circumstances – including those that seem unjust, ghastly, cruel and painful. Many people can't bring themselves to do this. It is the point where their prayers and their relationship with God breaks down. To thank him when we are in pain has to be a deliberate choice of faith, which says, 'Lord, I don't understand you, but I trust you. I thank you that out of this you will somehow bring good. I thank you that you are with me and you share my suffering. I thank you that in the end all will be well. I thank you that you said your grace will be sufficient for me' (2 Cor. 12:9). If you can't as yet say that, remember that it is OK to express your anger to God. It is better to express it than to keep repressing it. We know that God wants our hearts, that is to say, he wants our complete openness to him. When we let anger surface, he is there with us. He knows the causes of our anger. He can enable us to channel it in a direction which will not be destructive. To feel our anger is no sin. What we do with our anger is all-important. The world is full of injustices, some of which rightly make us very angry. They can and should spur us to action, because that anger is righteous i.e. right anger, as opposed to self-centred anger. What matters is to hold on to God by all means, even though it takes time, until we reach the point of being able to thank him.

Let me say again that we suffer from the hurts and pains of others as well as from our own. Some suffering is undeserved and some is brought on us by our own bad choices. And some suffering is to be seen as a part of God's individualised training programme for us. God tells us clearly that he himself disciplines us as his sons and daughters. In Hebrews 12:4–11 we read that he is disciplining us precisely because he is treating us as his children[9]. The choice is ours how we respond to discipline. In our suffering it is our thanksgiving, our sacrifice of praise, that brings Jesus closer to us. He saves us from self-pity and gives us joy and peace. What he bore for us exceeds all other pain. For us to carry our cross is, basically, to go on appropriating his life, come what may. As we thank him we can become a channel of his life, even in the midst of our suffering. Perhaps you know the last verse of this lovely hymn:

> Praise You, Lord,
> You have turned our thorns to roses,
> Glory, Lord,
> As they bloom upon your brow;
> The path of pain is hallowed,
> For Your love has made it sweet,
> Praise You, Lord, and may I love You now.[10]

Supplication

We move now to prayers which are requests and intercessions. Mostly our petitions will be for specific needs, which may be world needs, national needs, friends' needs, family needs. This is part of the second half of Jesus' great command to us. He says, 'Love your neighbour as you love yourself.' Loving yourself also means praying for your own personal needs as you perceive them. Loving your neighbour is praying for the one who is in trouble and is needing your love and help, and even more the love and healing of Jesus, through your prayers.

As you pray for someone, the Lord may well prompt you to do something practical, write a letter, go and visit, in some way be the Samaritan who will give help in that situation.

Praying for people is always closely linked with loving them. But if you have a prayer list of missionaries, church friends, and others whom you regularly pray for, you will know that your praying can sometimes become mechanical – just a routine. It's quite a common problem. Compassion can help you to pray. Most of all the love of Jesus in our hearts is needed. Often we don't have it because we don't ask for it. Pray for more love, and then go back to that list. God calls some people to a particular work of supplication and intercession. 'Watch and pray,' he instructs all his followers.

Lord Tennyson in his *Morte d'Arthur* has a beautiful reminder:

. . . .More things are wrought by prayer
Than this world dreams of. Wherefore, let thy voice
Rise like a fountain for me night and day.
For what are men better than sheep or goats
That nourish a blind life within the brain,
If, knowing God, they lift not hands of prayer
Both for themselves and those who call them friend?
For so the whole round earth is every way
Bound by gold chains about the feet of God.

Thank God for people who are giving time to the work of intercession. They are needed now perhaps more than they have ever been.

Out into the daily routine

Let me say again that this quiet time with Bible study and with prayer is as precious as gold. It has to be fought for. We noted, with Steve, that satanic pressure to let the habit slip is frequently a part of the struggle. We have to *be strong in the Lord and in his mighty power*. St Paul's words to his young colleague Timothy can encourage us too: 'God has not given us a spirit that keeps shrinking back, but a spirit which he powerfully enables, giving us love and integrity of mind' (2 Tim. 1:7 paraphrased). In contemporary Western secular culture the Bible has lost its authority, as we know, and is no longer often taught or viewed as part of our national heritage. We also know that in this generation we are the losers; that we have been robbed of what gives our life meaning, purpose, stability, love and self-control. The quiet time for Bible study and prayer is indeed precious as gold. Through it God restores to us true values, the moral absolutes we have lost, as we persevere in our friendship with Jesus Christ, and in our obedience to him. 'Back to basics' then takes on a clear and compelling meaning. Our time in the stillness equips us to join others in showing and telling the love of God to a world adrift from its moorings.

The face of the King

In Dr McIntyre's *Hidden Life of Prayer*[11] he asks the question, 'To what profit is it that we dwell in Jerusalem, if we do not see the King's face?' What is the good of being in our church congregations and keeping busy with our traditional activities without experiencing the open heaven of meeting with our God and really knowing him? An open heaven is a close personal relationship with God, not merely our external church activities and routines. Seeing our King's face has everything to do with learning from the gospel what Jesus's face is like. By faith we can see him, and the more we see, the more we marvel and worship and thank and love him. The question is how much do we really love him?

A few years ago a communist asked his Christian friend, 'Does Jesus Christ mean much to you?' His friend replied, 'Yes, I would say that Jesus Christ means much to me.' To which came the immediate reply, 'Then that just shows the difference between you and me, because communism means *everything* to me.'

That brief conversation highlights the main question in this book: the place that the Person of Jesus

Christ has in our lives. Does he mean *something* to us? Does he mean *much* to us? Or, does he mean *everything* to us? Is he the most important person in our thinking and planning, in our work and our hobbies, in our relationships . . . above all in our heart's affection and our love? Where does he come?

Many of us find in all honesty that though we want to love him with all our heart, all our soul, all our mind and all our strength, yet our love is not what it ought to be. It is not as wholehearted or resolute as we would wish. So much else clamours for our attention. We are fallen and needy human beings, still distanced from the wonder and loveliness of the Person himself. What will draw us closer? As we have already noted, practical James, the Apostle, comments: 'You don't have because you don't ask.' Do we *ask* to receive more of his love? The prime fruit of Jesus' Spirit is love. God wants to pour out much more love into our lives (see Romans 5:5). We note that the love some Christians have for Jesus Christ and also for his people has a great depth of reality and self-giving about it. Among my friends are several whose witness of love has been a tremendous incentive to me, and in this final chapter I would like to tell you about a few of them. In each case their love has grown from their habitual times in the stillness with the Lord.

She was ten years old

The first witness is an Indian girl, ten years old, who lived 50 years ago with her parents in a border village of Kashmir. The frontier between Muslims and Hindus had begun to be highly disputed. This girl and her parents became the target of a night-time attack, led by Chaudhry, a Kashmiri Muslim fighter, who later became my friend. At this stage he saw it as his duty to kill this family, even though they were Christians and not Hindus. In the light of an oil lamp he accosted the frightened parents. The girl then came out, completely fearless, and refused to deny Jesus Christ. She asked permission to pray a last prayer with her parents. Chaudhry sarcastically permitted this. They knelt and entrusted themselves to the One they knew who had promised to be with them to the end of the world. Their prayer finished, 'In the Name of the Lord Jesus Christ, Amen.'

As the word 'Amen' was uttered a wall of brilliant light rose out of the ground. This wall hid the three of them from the soldiers' sight. Although Chaudhry had been in the habit of playing with the deathly fire and flames of high explosives, he had never in all his life seen such a bright and terrifying light. It was unique, an ethereal sort of light which he was quite incapable of describing in words.

Gradually the light came closer and closer to him and he panicked. It seemed as if this light would advance and burn him up. He broke out in perspiration and began to dribble at the mouth. He didn't know what to do until suddenly the thought rose in his mind that he ought to apologise to those 'wretched creatures' and beg their forgiveness; so he said in fear and trembling, 'Please forgive me.' He said later that they were obviously in touch with a greater power than he had ever witnessed. He heard, 'We forgive you in the name of Jesus Christ.'

As soon as this sentence was uttered, the wall of fire vanished. They stood once more before the soldiers, peaceful and calm, ready to do whatever Chaudhry commanded. He and his men wouldn't stay there any longer. 'A little child will lead them' (Isa. 11:6) seemed so appropriate. That child loved Jesus Christ and believed his word.

This extraordinary incident haunted Chaudhry, a highly educated man. It became one of several happenings which convinced him in his own spiritual search. The little girl's 'Jesus Christ' had come and saved her at precisely the right moment, and Chaudhry had witnessed Christ's powerful protection with his own eyes. Not much later he turned over his life to Jesus and was renamed Ghulam Masih Naaman.[12]

A modern Barnabas

The second witness is Joseph Brown who was a skilled pattern-maker at Crompton Parkinson's electrical engineering firm in Chelmsford. His humble saintliness earned him the nickname 'Holy Joe'. His workmates knew him to be a man of prayer. Neither his character nor his language could be faulted. He never allowed himself to say anything negative about another person. Some tried to tease him or even menace him with aggressive words or behaviour, sometimes stealing his tools just to take the mickey out of him. But Joseph Brown was like his Master. *'When they hurled their insults at him, he did not retaliate'* (1 Pet. 2:23). He was an elder at Orchard Street Hall. His prayers, coming from his heart in the morning meeting, took us right into the presence of God. They expressed just what Jesus meant to him: 'everything'. He was never late for church, always present for the prayer meeting.

One of Joe Brown's great virtues was his gift of encouragement. I remember when elderly Mr Gooding lost his wife. The first person to come to his door was Joe Brown. He didn't say much, 'I just put my arms around his neck and wept and kissed him' Joe told me in tears. He cared deeply for people because the Lord Jesus was central in his life. Some years later I was privileged to conduct his funeral, and the nearest Bible character I could think of to match Joseph Brown's character was another Joseph, the Levite from Cyprus whom the apostles called Barnabas which means Son of Encouragement (Acts 4:36). That first Barnabas was generous with his money (Acts 4:37); he urged the apostles to accept the genuineness of Saul's recent conversion (Acts 9:27). He encouraged the new believers in Antioch to remain true to the Lord (Acts 11:23) He was glad when he saw evidence of the grace of God. Luke described him as a 'good man, full of the Holy Spirit and faith' (Acts 11:24). All those beautiful characteristics perfectly described Joe Brown. Yes, he was another of those lovers of Jesus whose face shone with the glory. The factory sobriquet 'Holy Joe' was so apt.

Undeterred to the end

The third witness is Mrs. Leys, lying in a London hospital bed with cancer of her throat. An opening had been made in her throat (a tracheostomy) to enable her to breathe. Every so often the tracheostomy tube would become blocked with mucus, her breathing would then become obstructed and she would become blue and in distress. The patient in the next bed would call a nurse if she had not already heard and seen Mrs. Leys struggling for breath. After the nurse had run across the ward and cleared the tube, Mrs. Leys wrote on her slate with a twinkle in her eye: 'You have just stopped me going to Heaven!' She had an amazing sense of humour and used to cheer up patients on her ward with little messages on the slate. She would send them words of encouragement and hope. She communicated God's love wherever she went. I had known her for a few years and recognised in her another lover of Jesus and a woman with a deep life of prayer. These three always seem to go together: a love for Jesus, a love for people, and a life of prayer.

Lover of the Afghans

Next I remember Christy Wilson. We first met up at Cambridge in 1949. We had a burden to pray for Afghanistan and both felt a calling to go there through whatever door the Lord would open for us. Christy was one of those men in whom you immediately recognise the presence of Christ. He was a man of love and a man of prayer. It was a joy to kneel down beside him and hear him open his heart for Afghans, begging the Lord to make a way into their country.

Our next meeting was in Peshawar in September 1966. Christy had already entered Afghanistan as a teacher of English in the prestigious Habibiah High School for young men. He was also recognised by the Afghan government as the pastor of the International Christian Church, the first ordained person to be granted a visa for such a role.

I soon saw that Christy was loved by the Afghans. The reasons were threefold. He spoke their language fluently and knew their culture well, having grown up in neighbouring Iran.[13] Secondly, he was a man of prayer, and for strict Muslims who pray five times a day, that was a considerable plus in their acceptance of him. Thirdly, he was also a man of love. He and his wife, Betty, both showed the same characteristics of prayer and love which opened up doors of influence for that couple in a country where Christianity was neither known, nor understood, nor wanted. In fact it was only known by the way it was depicted in Western, in other words 'Christian'(!) films, in 'Christian' dress (such as miniskirts!), 'Christian language', 'Christian' food, such as pork (horrors!) and alcohol – both forbidden in Islam. It was not until people like Christy and his wife came to the country prepared to adapt to Muslim culture that biblical Christianity became visible and acceptable.

Christy had an outstanding influence among the Afghans who came to recognise in him an authentic picture of Jesus Christ. He cared for them. Everybody in that country knew that Christy also loved Jesus. I remember a day when he and I arrived at a petrol station. He seemed to know the name of the man who filled up his tank. He asked him, 'How is your wife now? Is she better? No? I am so sorry. Let us pray for her.' With that he took off his hat and prayed briefly in Jesus' Name for the man's wife, that she would be healed. He replaced his Afghan hat, paid for his petrol and we drove off leaving a grateful Afghan wishing us God's blessing. It was no surprise to me how much time he quietly spent in prayer and fasting, interceding for the salvation of Afghans, and it was no surprise that they loved him so much.

A night-time visitation

Lastly let me tell you about one more of my friends, Michael. Michael was a doctor living in our home. He was tall and thin, highly intelligent and with a wonderful sense of humour. All the years I have known him I have seen his love for Jesus blossom and grow increasingly attractive and beautiful. His whole life has just glowed with it. We were working in a very busy mission hospital in Quetta, Baluchistan. One night he gently tapped on our bedroom door. 'Come in, Michael.' It was 4 a.m. He had not yet gone to bed. The hours since we had all prayed and said good-night to each other he had spent in prayer, seeking to be filled with the Holy Spirit. He simply said to us, 'I want you to know that I believe in the Holy Spirit.' His face shone with joy and our bedroom was filled with a sense of God's

Presence. My wife and I got on our knees to speak to the One who had met with our dear brother that night. He has always been one of those special lovers of Jesus whose life creates a great desire in the rest of us to open up our own hearts and lives to him in a more radical way. Michael has always sustained that love by making time, especially at the beginning of the day, to meet our Lord and cherish His presence.

Loving the King

The Lord's love does make all the difference. Thank God that in these secular post-modern, media-controlled days there is a growing number of people who are seeking God. There is also an increasing multitude of people young and old who have committed themselves to follow Jesus Christ. God has become their Heavenly Father, Jesus has become their Master, Saviour and Lord, and his Spirit is leading them. Their spiritual nourishment is the intake of God's Word, and the growing strength of their lives is the loving presence of God mediated to them through their praying.

I want to stress that the life that they foster and nourish in the stillness is no recluse's life. It is the very love of God, with their heart and soul and mind, which actually strengthens and motivates them to go out to their neighbours and labour on their behalf. The Quakers (or Friends) in their own way, with their unobtrusive international work of mediation, exemplify this, and so do many others, who live sacrificial caring lives, in the community and in the

In The Stillness

international scene. Jesus himself set the pattern. He called his first disciples to be *with* him, and only after that sent them to the work of God's kingdom (Mark 3:14). This kingdom life consists of going in to God and out to involvement in the community. We pray, 'Your kingdom come, your will be done on earth as in heaven.' This kingdom life, which contrasts so radically with the values of our Western culture, increasingly becomes our life when we set ourselves to love and serve the King. It is when we are out of touch with our King that our prayers become routine and stale and even imprisoning. Our receptiveness and our longing for him is always the doorway through which he comes. And then he can send us out again and again, empowered and equipped for the work of his kingdom. Not many of us can say that Jesus means everything to us. But we can taste and see, as we kneel before him. So let us humbly kneel, and taste again.

'To what profit is it that we dwell in Jerusalem, if we do not see the King's face?'[14]

Notes

1 See Acts 10:43.
2 'The Law, the Psalms (or Writings), and the Prophets' was a term meaning *all* the O T Scriptures.
3 Reference may also be made to the following verses: Gen. 28:18; Exod. 29:39,42,; 30:7; Ps. 5:3; 59:16.
4 Bletchley: Scripture Union 1998 Bletchley: Scripture Union 1985
5 For example, Autobiography of George Muller London: Pickering & Inglis 1929; *George Müller and his Orphans*, by Nancy Garton, London: Hodder & Stoughton 1964
6 Colarado Springs: Naupress 1993
7 Eph. 2:6; Col. 3:1
8 With the words, 'Jesus is Lord' Kay passed into Jesus' presence, September, 1998.
9 See also Revelation 3:19; John 15:2
10 Nettie Rose, *Thankyou Music*, 1977
11 D. M. McIntyre, Christian Focus Publication 1994
12 Ghulam Masih Naaman with Vita Toon, *The Unexpected Enemy* Basingstoke: Marshall

Pickering 1985 Marshall Morgan & Scott Ltd
1985
13 His parents had been missionaries there.
14 Dr McIntyre's *Hidden Life of Prayer*